WRITTEN AND ILLUSTRATED BY BONNIE SHEMIE

BUILDING CANADA

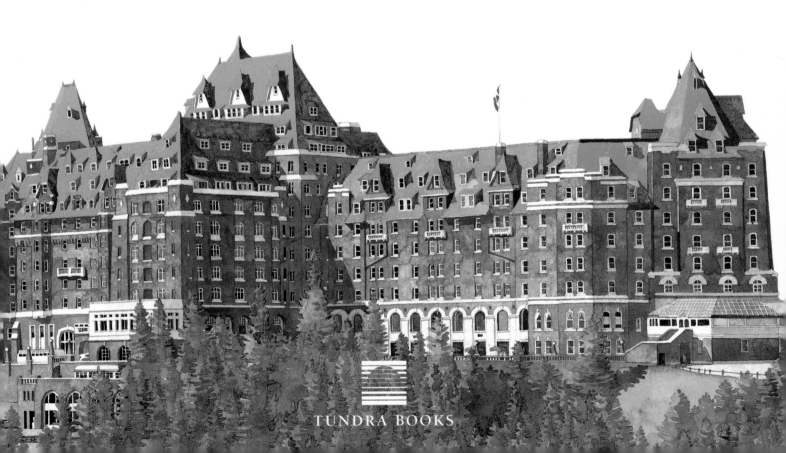

TUNDRA BOOKS

Published in Canada by Tundra Books,
481 University Avenue, Toronto, Ontario M5G 2E9

Published in the United States by Tundra Books of Northern New York,
P.O. Box 1030, Plattsburgh, New York 12901

Library of Congress Control Number: 00-135458

National Library of Canada Cataloguing in Publication Data

Shemie, Bonnie, 1949-
   Building Canada

ISBN 0-88776-504-1

1. Architecture – Canada – History – Juvenile literature. I. Title.

NA740.S53 2001   j720'.971   C00-932280-9

We acknowledge the support of the Canada Council for the Arts and the Ontario Arts Council for
our publishing program.

We acknowledge the financial support of the Government of Canada through the Book Publishing
Industry Development Program for our publishing activities.

Design: Sari Ginsberg

Medium: watercolour on paper

Printed in Hong Kong, China

2 3 4 5 6   06 05 04 03 02

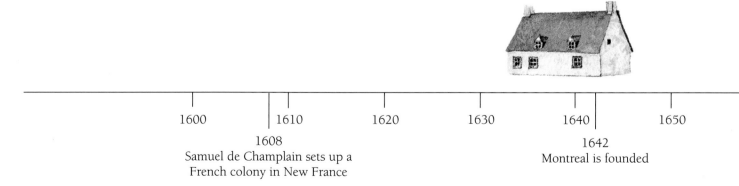

1600   1610   1620   1630   1640   1650

1608
Samuel de Champlain sets up a
French colony in New France

1642
Montreal is founded

To the memory of my parents,
Eva Louise and William Brenner, Jr.

| 1660 | 1670 | 1680 | 1690 | 1700 | 1710 | 1720 |

1713
The Treaty of Utrecht is signed, and
France cedes Newfoundland and
most of the original French colony
of Acadia to Britain

ACKNOWLEDGEMENTS

I am deeply indebted to the following: the work of Harold Kalman, specifically his *History of Canadian Architecture,* vols. 1 and 2 (Toronto: Oxford University Press, 1995), as well as to the work of the many other wonderful architectural historians who write about Canada; the libraries of McGill University, Concordia University, and the Canadian Centre for Architecture; the Canadian Inventory of Historic Buildings (Department of Canadian Heritage); Parks Canada; the Ministry of Citizenship, Culture and Recreation of Ontario; the Public Archives and the Department of Tourism of Prince Edward Island; the Provincial Archives of Manitoba; the British Columbia Archives; the Canadian Pacific Archives; Dr. David Lai, University of Victoria, for sharing his knowledge about Chinatown in Victoria; the architect James Aitken, for his advice; the architect Alain Fournier, for information about housing in the North; Dane Lanken, for information about the Empress Theatre; and the offices of Paul Merrick Architects Ltd. and Maurer Kobayashi Architects Ltd., for providing information and visuals about those of their buildings that appear in this book.

Special thanks are owed to Janice Weaver for her fine editing job. And I especially acknowledge the faith, advice, and support of my publisher, Kathy Lowinger, and her staff at Tundra.

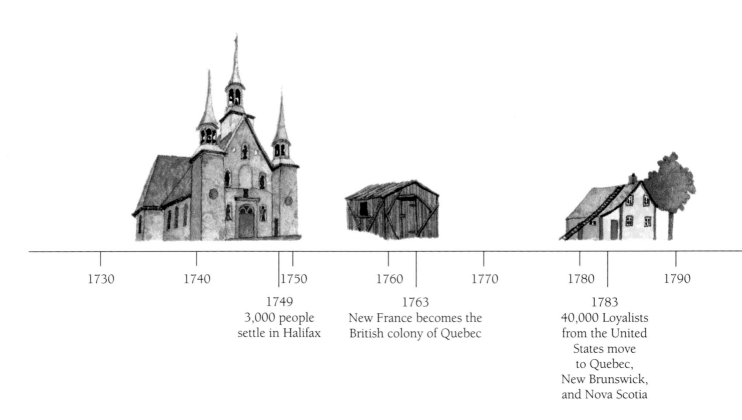

| 1730 | 1740 | 1750 | 1760 | 1770 | 1780 | 1790 |

1749
3,000 people
settle in Halifax

1763
New France becomes the
British colony of Quebec

1783
40,000 Loyalists
from the United
States move
to Quebec,
New Brunswick,
and Nova Scotia

CONTENTS

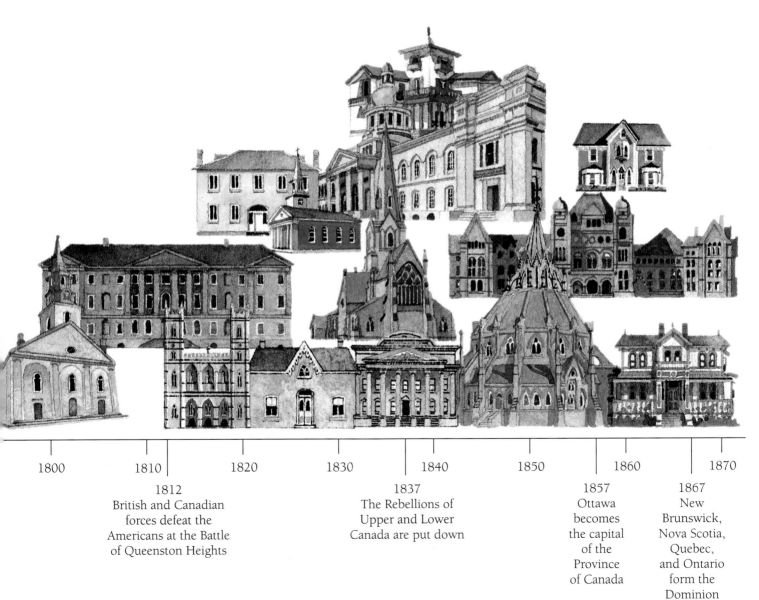

1800   1810   1820   1830   1840   1850   1860   1870

1812
British and Canadian
forces defeat the
Americans at the Battle
of Queenston Heights

1837
The Rebellions of
Upper and Lower
Canada are put down

1857
Ottawa
becomes
the capital
of the
Province
of Canada

1867
New
Brunswick,
Nova Scotia,
Quebec,
and Ontario
form the
Dominion
of Canada

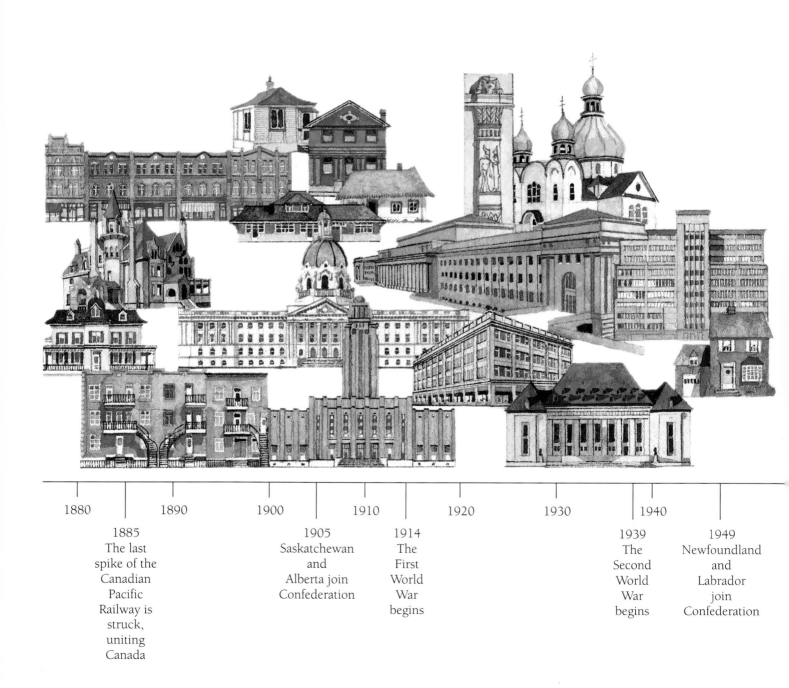

1880   1890   1900   1910   1920   1930   1940

1885
The last
spike of the
Canadian
Pacific
Railway is
struck,
uniting
Canada

1905
Saskatchewan
and
Alberta join
Confederation

1914
The
First
World
War
begins

1939
The
Second
World
War
begins

1949
Newfoundland
and
Labrador
join
Confederation

INTRODUCTION

H ave you ever been in a city, surrounded by rushing people and lights and noise, and looked up and been surprised by the silent, soaring buildings above you? Have you ever been impressed by a beautiful carving on an elevator door or an intricate design on a tile floor? Have you ever looked out your window on a fearsomely stormy winter night and wondered how people survived hundreds of years ago?

The buildings we make not only shelter us, but also are very close to our feelings. They can be places of refuge or public gathering spaces; they can declare our national identity or our financial might; they can even be an inspiring art form. This short history of architecture in Canada, which begins with Samuel de Champlain's establishment of the first habitations in Quebec and ends with our postmodern buildings of today, describes the forces that shape the buildings around us.

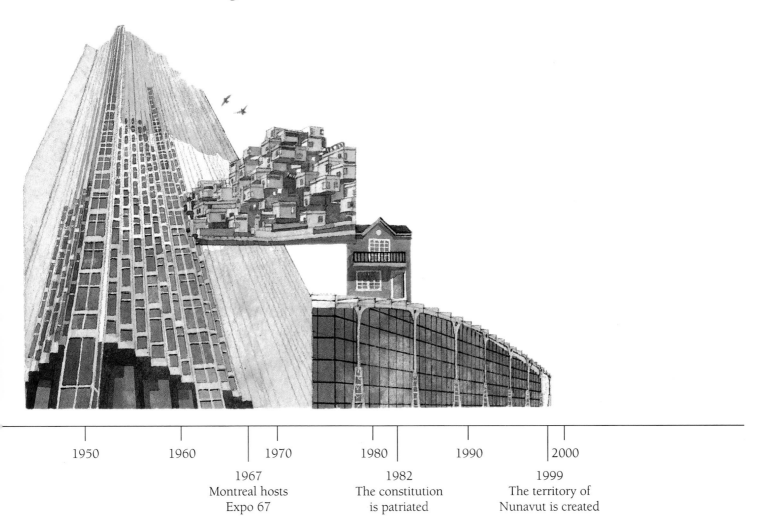

1950	1960	1970	1980	1990	2000

1967
Montreal hosts
Expo 67

1982
The constitution
is patriated

1999
The territory of
Nunavut is created

The French, who arrived in the early 1600s, were the first European settlers to bring their culture to Canadian soil. Like all newcomers, they tried to reproduce familiar surroundings in a strange new land. Their first cottages were similar to those they left behind in France – simple rectangles made of stone or wood, with steeply pitched roofs sometimes pierced by dormer windows. Because the winter was a lot colder here than in France, the settlers built thicker walls, added shutters, and raised the first floor away from the deep snow. Sometimes the roof was extended out to form a porch (or gallery). The *maison Canadienne,* as this house style came to be called, is still dear to French Canadians and remains popular today.

Houses built in the three major cities of the time (Quebec, Trois-Rivières, and Montreal) kept the same basic design but were several storeys high. To prevent the spread of fire, politicians of the day developed building regulations.

These included the building of firebreaks, thick gables that rose above the roofline between buildings. But despite these regulations, fires such as the one in 1852, which consumed the homes of one-fifth of the population of Montreal, continued to be a serious threat.

The French settlers were cut off from France by the British conquest of 1759–60, but they kept their traditions and maintained their distinct French-Canadian building style. This style can be seen most obviously in the parish church, which has followed much the same design into this century. The tin roofs and magnificent steeples still rise above the welter of buildings in towns and villages all over Quebec. Simple and austere on the outside, these churches are a surprise on the inside because of their rich carvings and colourfully painted walls.

Girardin House (Beauport, Quebec, 1650–70) was built like thousands of houses in northern and central France, but a lime wash called *crépi* was spread over the walls to protect the mortar joints between the stones from the repeated freezing and thawing that was unavoidable in the extreme Canadian climate.

Notre-Dame-des-Victoires (Quebec City, 1688) and **Place Royale** (reconstructed in the 1960s to look as it did in the late 1700s) were extensively damaged during the two-month British siege of Quebec in 1760.

Maison Ouimet (Laval, Quebec, 1735–43) shows the adaptations settlers made to survive the cold Canadian winters.

After England won the Seven Years' War in 1760, the British government encouraged large numbers of Protestants to establish themselves in Canada to balance the influence of the French Catholics. With the start of the American Revolution in 1775, colonists who were loyal to the British king joined these new settlers north of the border.

Admiration of English institutions led the wealthy to build large houses in the Georgian style (named for the four British monarchs called George who ruled between 1714 and 1830). Georgian buildings are characterized by perfect symmetry and order, and are often decorated with classical ornaments copied from ancient Greek architecture. In the United States, the Georgian style fell out of fashion after the revolution because it was associated with colonial oppression. Not so in Canada, where remnants of this style were used in public buildings up to the 1920s.

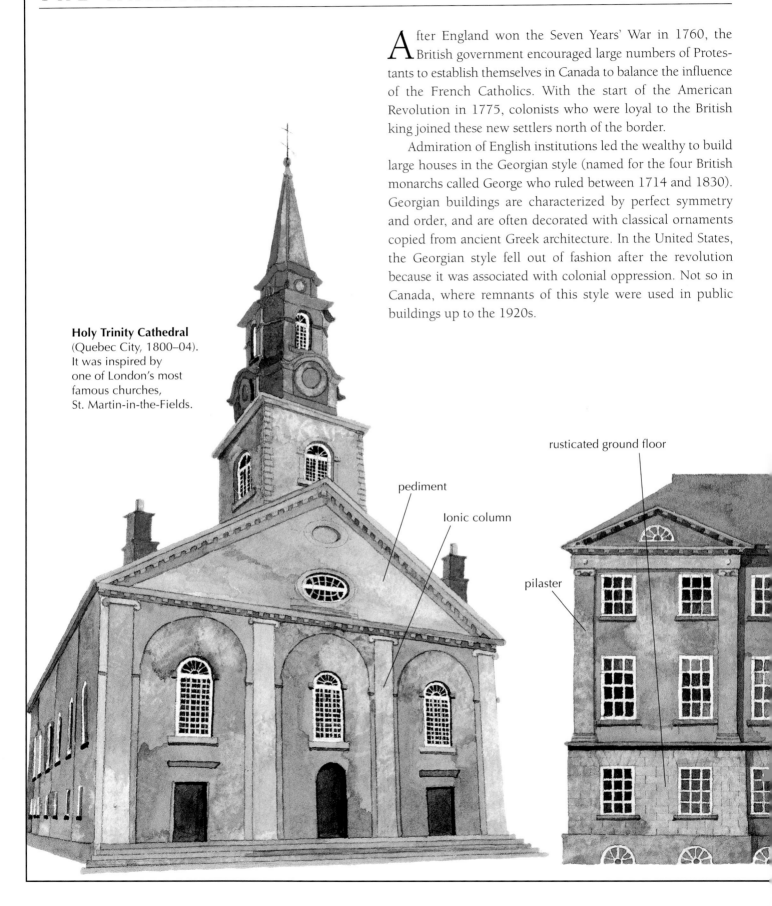

Holy Trinity Cathedral (Quebec City, 1800–04). It was inspired by one of London's most famous churches, St. Martin-in-the-Fields.

pediment

Ionic column

rusticated ground floor

pilaster

The first dwellings of new settlers provided only basic shelter. Walls were made of round or squared-off logs. Sometimes, homes were little more than a row of sticks placed upright in a trench, as in the **Newfoundland "tilt."**

This Newfoundland wood house is typical of the period between 1650 and 1850. As soon as settlers became more established, they built homes with saw-cut wood and kept the original cabin as a shed. Houses were painted with bright colours so they could be seen from the sea.

Below: **Maplelawn** (Ottawa, c.1831–34). As Maplelawn demonstrates, a well-designed Georgian house is always perfectly symmetrical.

Below: **Province House** (Halifax, 1811–18). Considered one of the finest Georgian buildings in Canada, Province House exhibits a characteristic common to public Georgian buildings: a rusticated ground floor (that is, with rough surface stonework) with smooth walls above.

portico

each storey clearly defined

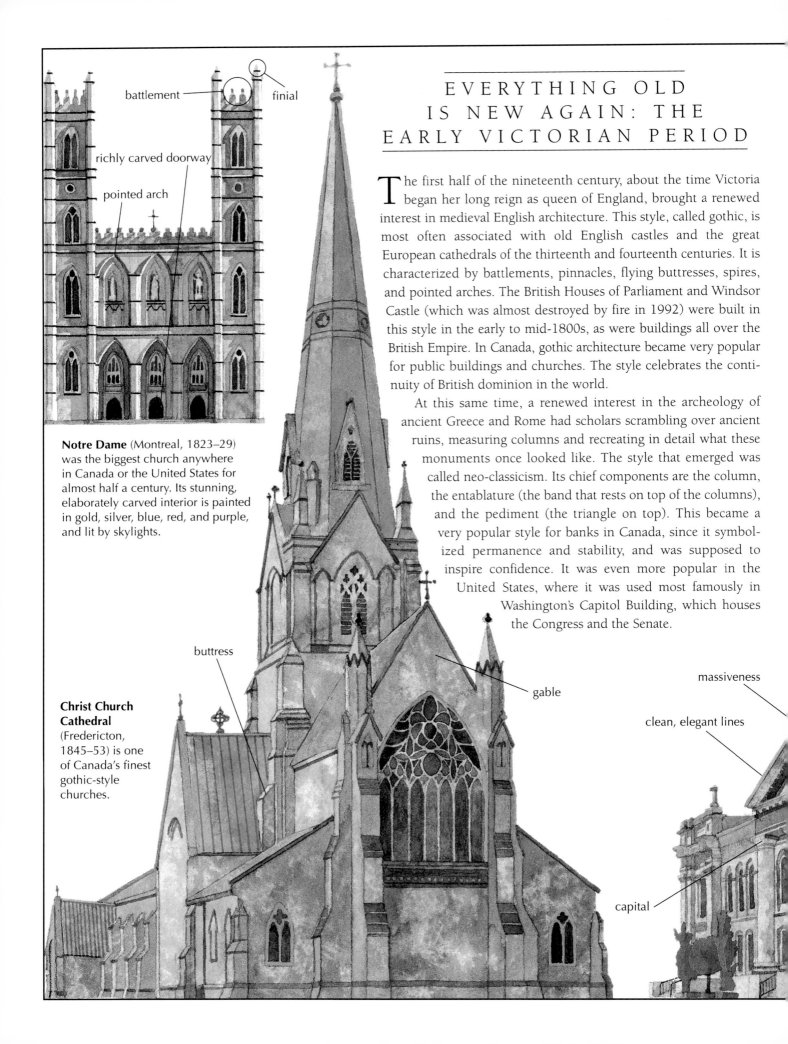

battlement

finial

richly carved doorway

pointed arch

Notre Dame (Montreal, 1823–29) was the biggest church anywhere in Canada or the United States for almost half a century. Its stunning, elaborately carved interior is painted in gold, silver, blue, red, and purple, and lit by skylights.

buttress

Christ Church Cathedral (Fredericton, 1845–53) is one of Canada's finest gothic-style churches.

gable

massiveness

clean, elegant lines

capital

EVERYTHING OLD IS NEW AGAIN: THE EARLY VICTORIAN PERIOD

The first half of the nineteenth century, about the time Victoria began her long reign as queen of England, brought a renewed interest in medieval English architecture. This style, called gothic, is most often associated with old English castles and the great European cathedrals of the thirteenth and fourteenth centuries. It is characterized by battlements, pinnacles, flying buttresses, spires, and pointed arches. The British Houses of Parliament and Windsor Castle (which was almost destroyed by fire in 1992) were built in this style in the early to mid-1800s, as were buildings all over the British Empire. In Canada, gothic architecture became very popular for public buildings and churches. The style celebrates the continuity of British dominion in the world.

At this same time, a renewed interest in the archeology of ancient Greece and Rome had scholars scrambling over ancient ruins, measuring columns and recreating in detail what these monuments once looked like. The style that emerged was called neo-classicism. Its chief components are the column, the entablature (the band that rests on top of the columns), and the pediment (the triangle on top). This became a very popular style for banks in Canada, since it symbolized permanence and stability, and was supposed to inspire confidence. It was even more popular in the United States, where it was used most famously in Washington's Capitol Building, which houses the Congress and the Senate.

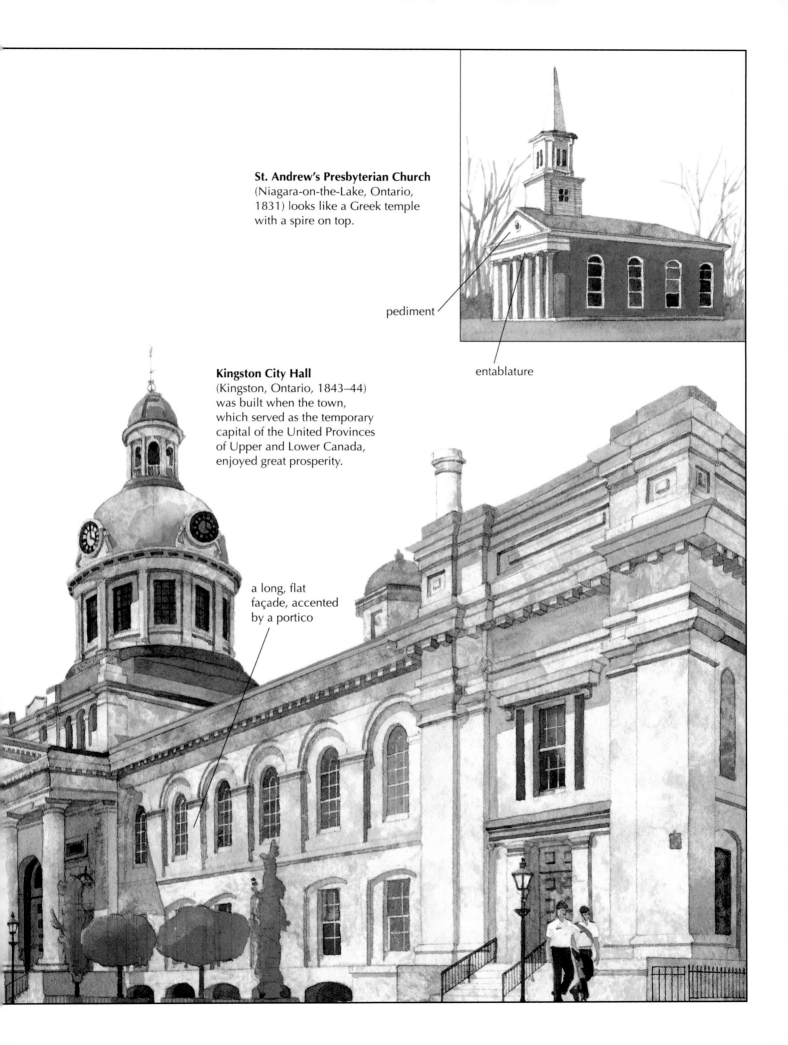

St. Andrew's Presbyterian Church
(Niagara-on-the-Lake, Ontario, 1831) looks like a Greek temple with a spire on top.

pediment

entablature

Kingston City Hall
(Kingston, Ontario, 1843–44) was built when the town, which served as the temporary capital of the United Provinces of Upper and Lower Canada, enjoyed great prosperity.

a long, flat façade, accented by a portico

HEADING WEST

The frontier kept moving westward as posts for the fur trade and farming settlements were established. The most important of these was the Red River Settlement in what is now southern Manitoba. It was settled by Scottish, English- and French-speaking Canadians, and Métis (people of mixed Native and French ancestry).

The West Coast was isolated from the rest of Canada by the Rocky Mountains. As a result, building styles there were influenced primarily by American settlements directly to the south. But there were other influences as well. Between 1881 and 1884, thousands of Chinese came to Canada to work on the Canadian Pacific Railway. Many later settled in Vancouver and Victoria. In fact, Victoria's three thousand Chinese lived in the four-block area that became Chinatown. Settlers brought with them their own distinct building traditions from China.

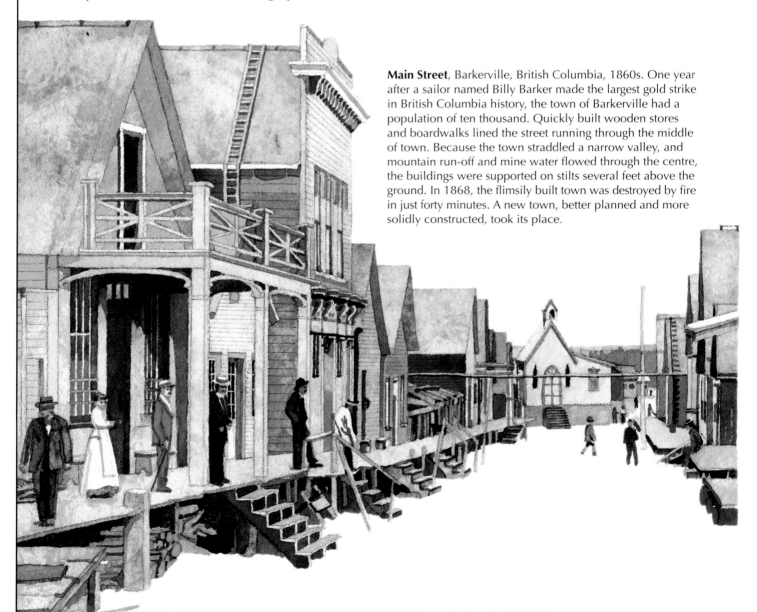

Main Street, Barkerville, British Columbia, 1860s. One year after a sailor named Billy Barker made the largest gold strike in British Columbia history, the town of Barkerville had a population of ten thousand. Quickly built wooden stores and boardwalks lined the street running through the middle of town. Because the town straddled a narrow valley, and mountain run-off and mine water flowed through the centre, the buildings were supported on stilts several feet above the ground. In 1868, the flimsily built town was destroyed by fire in just forty minutes. A new town, better planned and more solidly constructed, took its place.

Opposite: Both Natives and Europeans struggled for control over the junction of the Red and Assiniboine rivers, the gateway to the West. **Lower Fort Garry** was one of the forts established here.

Richard Carr House (Victoria, 1863). Modelled on two designs found in an American pattern book of 1852, this was the childhood home of a famous Canadian painter, Emily Carr.

Mennonite House-Barn. The Mennonites, who were seeking religious freedom in Canada and settled mostly in present-day Manitoba, brought from Europe this very old traditional design. The house is attached to the stable, which is built a little higher and wider.

These three buildings – the **Lung Kong Kung Shaw Society** (left), the **Chinese Empire Reform Society** (middle), and the **Tam Kung Temple** (right, demolished 1912) – in Victoria's Chinatown are made distinct by their balconies, a style imported from warm southern China.

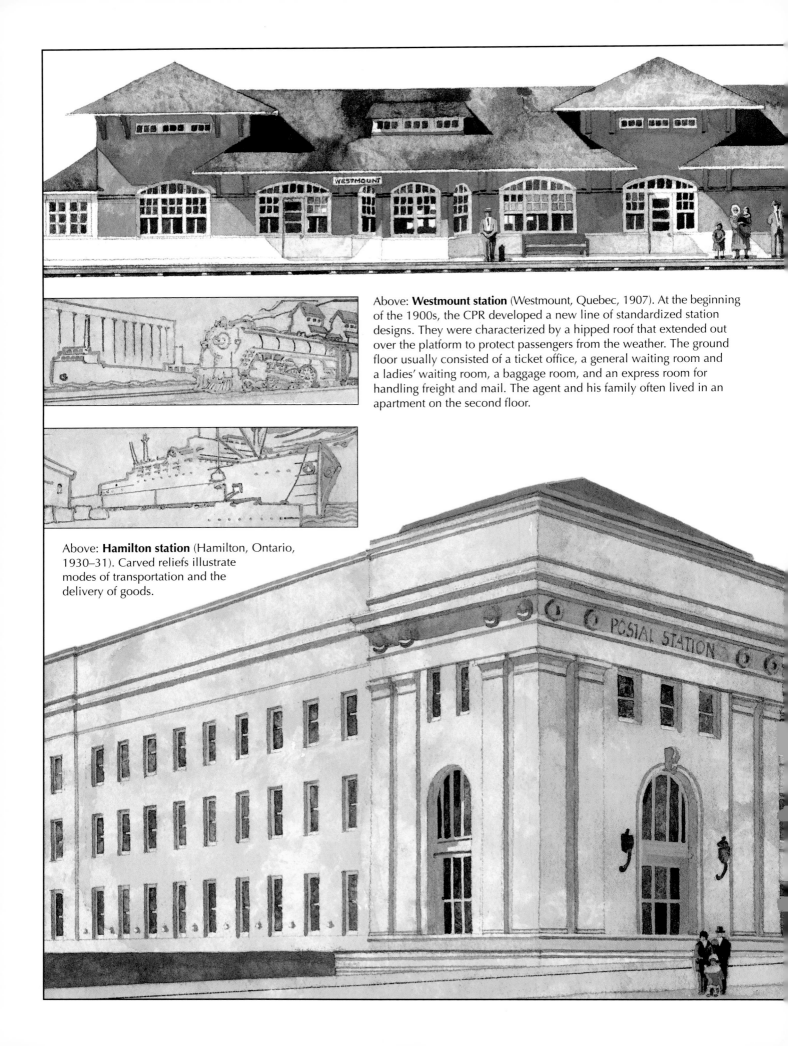

Above: **Westmount station** (Westmount, Quebec, 1907). At the beginning of the 1900s, the CPR developed a new line of standardized station designs. They were characterized by a hipped roof that extended out over the platform to protect passengers from the weather. The ground floor usually consisted of a ticket office, a general waiting room and a ladies' waiting room, a baggage room, and an express room for handling freight and mail. The agent and his family often lived in an apartment on the second floor.

Above: **Hamilton station** (Hamilton, Ontario, 1930–31). Carved reliefs illustrate modes of transportation and the delivery of goods.

THE RAILWAY UNITES
THE DOMINION

Indian Head station (Indian Head, Saskatchewan, *c.* 1882). In the Prairies, railway stations became town meeting halls and were used to send telegraphs, receive mail-order parcels, and as gathering places.

In 1867, Nova Scotia and New Brunswick joined Quebec and Ontario to form the Dominion of Canada, an event we call Confederation. Manitoba, the North-West Territory, British Columbia, and Prince Edward Island joined within a few years. To bind this huge new country together, the railway was built. (In fact, the completion of the transcontinental railway was a condition of B.C.'s entry into Confederation.) By 1886, Montreal was linked to Vancouver via the Canadian Pacific Railway.

The CPR had the enormous task of building stations every thirteen kilometres (eight miles) along the five-thousand-kilometre (three-thousand-mile) track. (Thirteen kilometres was as far as a steam engine could go without needing more water.) These CPR stations – and those of competing railway companies – were the heart of large and small towns all across the West.

With several kilometres of train platforms, **Union Station** in Toronto (1914–30) was the biggest terminal in Canada. The middle section, which is supported by twenty-two massive pillars, contains a splendid twenty-seven-metre (eighty-eight-foot) ticket lobby with four-storey windows at each end.

hipped roof

A STYLE OF OUR OWN

As competition grew between the different railway lines, hotels were built to encourage passengers to stop not just in the big cities but in some smaller communities along the route. The Banff Springs Hotel (1911–28) offers views of some of most spectacular scenery in the country. Its steep hipped roofs, dormers, turrets, bay windows, and balconies exhibit a uniquely Canadian mix of styles, called the Canadian château style. This world-class railway hotel, and others like it, remains a famous landmark in the Canadian landscape even today.

dormer

balcony

This one-room cabin is typical of the kind of prefab that could be ordered from a catalogue.

A well-made sod house had walls more than half a metre (two feet) thick, was snug in winter, and turned green in summer. But it was said that one day of rain on the prairies was followed by three days of rain in the house.

LIFE ON THE PRAIRIES

Settlement of the West began in earnest at the very end of the 1800s. This was also the beginning of the industrial era. Mail-order homes, made of machine-sawn lumber and prefabricated ornamentation, arrived by train in communities from Manitoba to British Columbia.

The trains also brought new settlers in search of more and better land, European immigrants looking for new opportunities, and minority groups seeking religious freedom. For homesteaders who had no money to purchase supplies, the only available building material in the treeless prairies was sod. It proved to be an excellent solution to the cold, windy prairie winters, however, because of the grassland turf's high insulation values.

Stores were built with false "boom town" fronts (large parapets that hid the roof and made the stores look bigger and more solid than they really were). But the most prominent prairie building form was the grain elevator. A town's importance was measured by the number of elevators – as in "a three-elevator town."

Canadian Bank of Commerce (Creston, B.C., 1907). The components of this prefabricated bank could be shipped in two railway boxcars. Available in three sizes, buildings like this one could be assembled in a day.

This Ukrainian home followed centuries-old folk traditions. Roofs framed with poplar poles and thatched with prairie grass sloped to shed rain. Log walls were plastered with a mixture of mud, straw, animal dung, and lime.

The onion-shaped dome on **St. Julien Ukrainian Church** in Edmonton echoes the domed Byzantine churches of the sixth century.

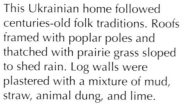

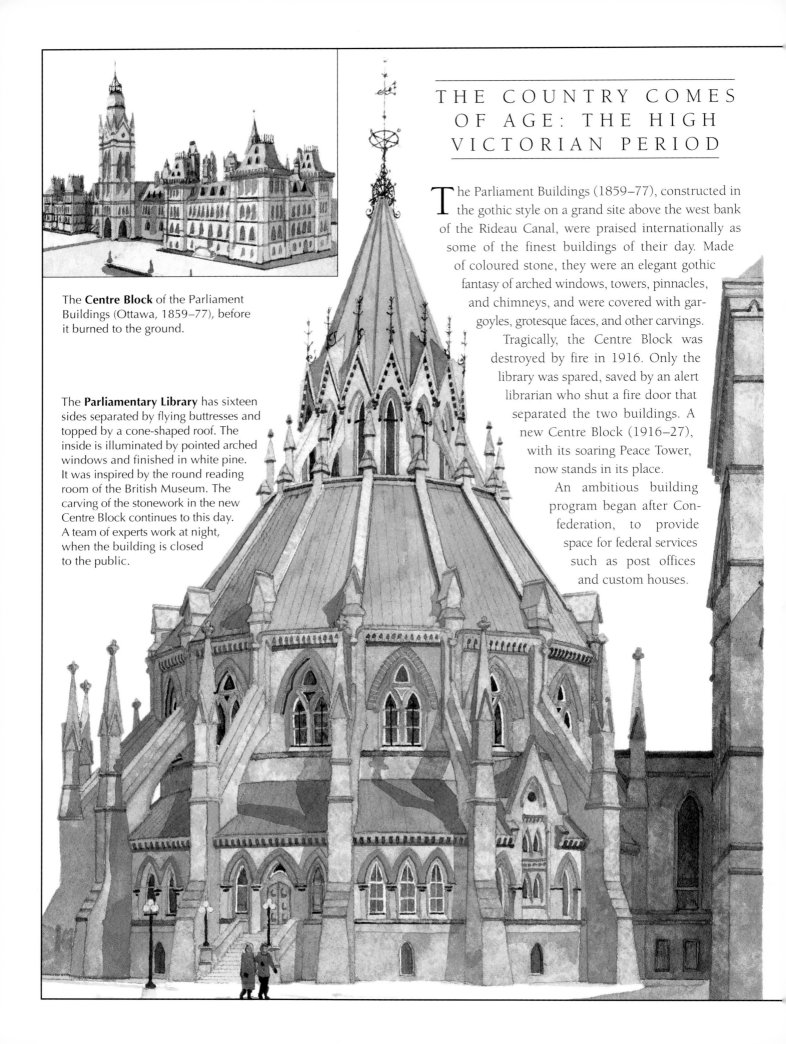

THE COUNTRY COMES OF AGE: THE HIGH VICTORIAN PERIOD

The **Centre Block** of the Parliament Buildings (Ottawa, 1859–77), before it burned to the ground.

The **Parliamentary Library** has sixteen sides separated by flying buttresses and topped by a cone-shaped roof. The inside is illuminated by pointed arched windows and finished in white pine. It was inspired by the round reading room of the British Museum. The carving of the stonework in the new Centre Block continues to this day. A team of experts work at night, when the building is closed to the public.

The Parliament Buildings (1859–77), constructed in the gothic style on a grand site above the west bank of the Rideau Canal, were praised internationally as some of the finest buildings of their day. Made of coloured stone, they were an elegant gothic fantasy of arched windows, towers, pinnacles, and chimneys, and were covered with gargoyles, grotesque faces, and other carvings. Tragically, the Centre Block was destroyed by fire in 1916. Only the library was spared, saved by an alert librarian who shut a fire door that separated the two buildings. A new Centre Block (1916–27), with its soaring Peace Tower, now stands in its place.

An ambitious building program began after Confederation, to provide space for federal services such as post offices and custom houses.

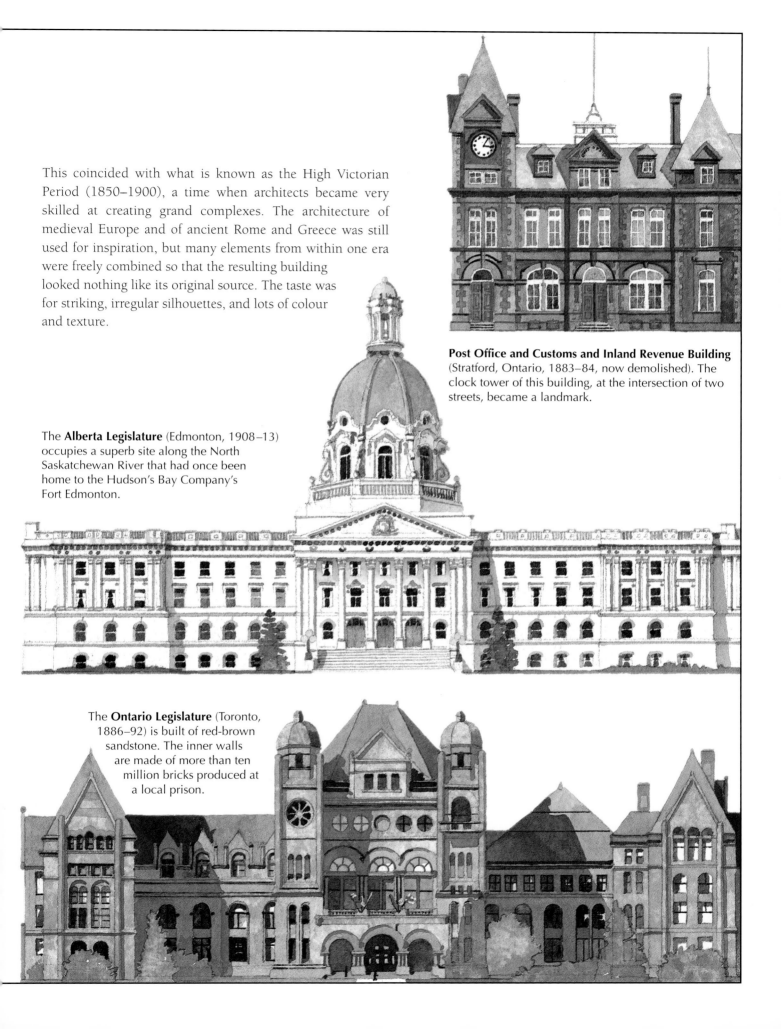

This coincided with what is known as the High Victorian Period (1850–1900), a time when architects became very skilled at creating grand complexes. The architecture of medieval Europe and of ancient Rome and Greece was still used for inspiration, but many elements from within one era were freely combined so that the resulting building looked nothing like its original source. The taste was for striking, irregular silhouettes, and lots of colour and texture.

Post Office and Customs and Inland Revenue Building (Stratford, Ontario, 1883–84, now demolished). The clock tower of this building, at the intersection of two streets, became a landmark.

The **Alberta Legislature** (Edmonton, 1908–13) occupies a superb site along the North Saskatchewan River that had once been home to the Hudson's Bay Company's Fort Edmonton.

The **Ontario Legislature** (Toronto, 1886–92) is built of red-brown sandstone. The inner walls are made of more than ten million bricks produced at a local prison.

This **Hudson's Bay Company** store in Victoria, built in 1922, is nearly identical to the company's stores in Vancouver and Calgary. The Corinthian columns separating the window bays give the four-storey building a stately appearance.

horizontal band between storeys

round or segmented arched window

In the late nineteenth century, cities across Canada bustled with commercial activity. Shops lined the main roads, which were often called King Street or Queen Street, and occupied the first floor of three- or four-storey walk-ups. Storage, offices, and residences were above. Victoria Row in Charlottetown is a well-preserved example of such a business district. The architectural style most often chosen by merchants was known as Victorian Italianate; it was inspired by buildings designed during the Italian Renaissance. Banks were usually modelled on the classical Greek temple, as they had been since the early 1800s. As they became more prosperous, the banks built splendid limestone and granite head offices in all major Canadian cities.

As land in urban areas became more and more valuable, two technological advances pushed buildings higher. The first was the fabrication, by the Otis company, of safe elevators. The second was the use of a cast-iron frame to carry the weight of the building. Exterior walls, known as curtain walls, then became only a shell that simply protected the interior from weather.

The head office of the **Bank of Montreal** (Montreal, 1845–48) has a six-column Corinthian portico and a magnificent banking hall, at one time said to be the largest in the world.

Victoria Row, Charlottetown

elaborate cornice

fanlight

pediment

entablature

pilaster

boldly decorated
cornice

Houses not only provide us with basic shelter from the elements, but also reflect our way of life and our status in society. The houses of the very rich are usually built in one of the popular styles of the time, using the services of an architect. It is fun to look at them to see the many variations that have developed in the past two centuries. The Poplars (Grafton, Ontario, 1817), at left, takes its inspiration from a Greek temple.

gable with decorated bargeboard

steeply pitched roof

pointed arched opening

The pointed arched windows of the **Burpee House** (Saint John, 1865) show gothic influence. Fine decorative woodwork has been added beneath the eaves and around the doors and windows.

wide eaves with
decorative bracket

projecting square tower

belvedere

low-pitched hip roof

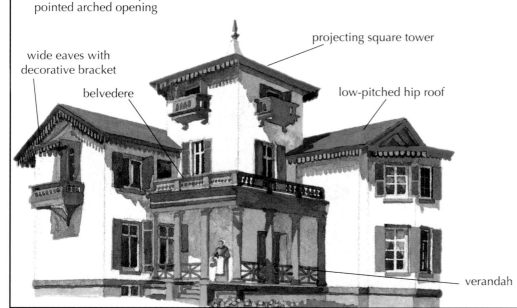

verandah

Picturesque **Bellevue** (Kingston, Ontario, 1843), probably the first villa in Canada in the Italianate style, caused quite a stir at the time it was built. Its most famous inhabitant was Sir John A. Macdonald, the future prime minister. He lived there with his family when he was thirty-three.

Birchwood (Charlottetown, 1877) is built in the Second Empire Style, which was made popular by Napoleon III and his beautiful queen, Eugenie, when they completed the construction of the Louvre in this style, in Paris in 1857.

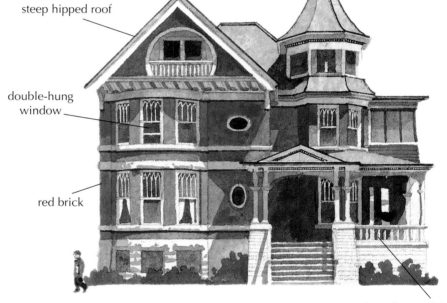

projecting centre tower

delicate filigree

dormer window

eaves with decorative bracket

Mansard roof

wrap-around verandah

Belcher House (Winnipeg, 1901) was built in the Queen Anne style. Though Queen Anne reigned in England from 1702–14, the style was revived in the late nineteenth century. Queen Anne houses were often large and irregularly shaped, with two or more storeys. The style was especially well suited for country manor houses.

steep hipped roof

double-hung window

red brick

broad verandah

Opulent **Craigdarroch Castle** (Victoria, 1887-90) is built in the château style, which is easily identified by the asymmetrical, castle-like silhouette and the heavy stone walls. Sadly, its owner, the coal baron Robert Dunsmuir, didn't live to see the house completed.

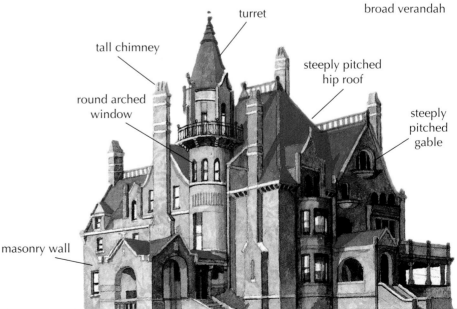

turret

tall chimney

steeply pitched hip roof

round arched window

steeply pitched gable

masonry wall

OUR HOMES

In the middle of the nineteenth century, as ordinary Canadians prospered, illustrated books showing designs for small and mid-size houses became popular. Plans were copied and changed to suit budgets and available materials. One design, used for Ontario farmhouses between 1860 and 1880, was unique to Canada. Built of brick, stone, or wood, the farmhouse always had one central gable crowning the front door. Kitchens were usually tacked onto the back, and the front door was used only for weddings and funerals.

As more and more people moved to the cities, real estate soared in value; costs were kept down by the creation of smaller lots, and duplexes and triplexes allowed more than one family to occupy the same piece of land. Montreal and Quebec City became famous for their flat-top duplexes, with their painted metal, spiral staircases. But the ultimate solution to high-density urban housing was the apartment building. First built around the end of the 1800s, apartment buildings survive in a multitude of forms to this day.

Based on plans published in the popular *Canadian Farmer* magazine, the "Ontario cottage" took Canada by storm.

Montreal duplexes have outside staircases to save on heating and construction costs. Though considered picturesque now, the staircases were pronounced an eyesore by many when they were first built.

1

2

3

1. New highways and public transportation allowed homes to be built farther from town and work, where the land was cheaper. This is a typical 1930s design.

2. In the booming post–Second World War economy, the average family could afford a car, and so built their dream home in the suburbs.

3. In the 1990s, designers at McGill University developed a "grow home," an affordable row-house that can be expanded as the family grows up.

Right: **Habitat 67** was an experiment in housing developed for Montreal's Expo 67. Its architect, Moshe Safdie, designed a system whereby concrete cubes could be stacked on top of one another by means of a crane. The plan aimed to provide housing for many people in a small space while maintaining privacy and variation in design.

After much experimentation, houses like this one in Great Whale, Quebec, were found to work best in the Far North. The severe cold causes the ground to be permanently frozen (except in the summer, when the top few inches thaw). The foundations of a house built on this type of ground will heave when the ground softens. Therefore, the structure is raised off the ground on stilts. The earth under the house is left intact, together with its insulating cover of moss. Trucks deliver fresh water and fuel and pick up waste water using a service entrance at the side of the house.

The stately **Supreme Court of Canada** (Ottawa, 1938-39) is an elegant example of modern classicism. The château-style roof was meant to unify the courthouse and other federal buildings.

BUILDING BETWEEN THE WARS

The twentieth century opened into an age of advanced machinery, available electricity, rapid transportation, and sophisticated communication. Old-style designs continued to be built, but now they were stripped down, simplified, and subdued, as with the Supreme Court of Canada. Modern reinforced concrete and steel girders, well hidden under traditional finishes, allowed buildings to soar ever higher.

Restraint was not the order of the day in the first "picture palaces." Movie chains tried to outdo each other in creating the most fabulous and unforgettable showplaces. The most exotic was Montreal's Empress Theatre, which was designed using an Egyptian theme (inspired by the discovery of Tutankhamen's tomb in 1922). The exterior featured lotus columns, sphinx heads, winged scarabs, and carved friezes. The inside was designed to look like the courtyard of an Egyptian palace.

Most of the interior decoration of the **Empress Theatre** (Montreal, 1927-28) was lost in a fire, but the building is being given new life as restoration work transforms it into a performing arts and multimedia centre.

1

2

3

ART DECO DAZZLE

Not all buildings of the early 1900s looked back to the Victorian era, but nor did they yet make a complete break with the past (as would be required by the modern movement). In the 1920s, a decorative movement that began in France spread to North America. It was called Art Deco. Inspired by both the clean lines of the new automobile designs and the music of the jazz age, this style is characterized by elegant simplicity, smooth geometric angles, curves, chevrons, zigzags, and pastel colours.

1. Decorations above the main entrance to the **Marine Building** show Canada geese flying across the rays of the sun.

2. **Eaton**'s Art Deco dining room (1925–27) is located on the ninth floor of the Montreal store. The room is eleven metres (thirty-five feet) high and lit by windows of opal glass. A large mural dominates one end.

3. Part of a frieze above the first floor of the **Marine Building** (Vancouver, 1929–30) shows a sea horse, plants, and waves. The building was constructed to house offices for the shipping industry.

4. The **University of Montreal**, designed by Ernst Cormier, has an exterior curtain wall of beige brick that covers a reinforced concrete structure.

4

THE MODERN AGE

As we reached the midway point of the 1900s, traditional designs continued to be built, but a new generation of architects set out to break with the past and develop a whole new way of looking at things. They wanted buildings that were simple, efficient, and used plain but modern materials (such as concrete, glass, steel, and aluminum). And modern buildings were "distinctive" in another way: they looked the same anywhere in the world.

The best modernist buildings have a crisp, clear orderliness. Fuelled by the economic boom that followed the Second World War, cities began competing to have the highest skyscraper, a quest that changed Canadian city skylines radically.

But within fifteen years, this stern minimalism began to feel cold and aloof. Cities strained with traffic problems, and hordes of people gathered downtown in the daytime but abandoned it at night. Architects soon realized that they had to work with city planners to create friendlier office environments. They began to pay attention to circulation patterns, and created lively indoor spaces and glassed-in atriums that kept out the elements but let in the outside light. The atrium of the Law Court in Vancouver's Robson Square, designed by Arthur Erickson, is pictured below.

Designers also began to bend the rules and become more dramatic and expressive. Towers were no longer dull rectangular boxes, but began to be designed to look more sculptured. The Royal Bank Plaza (built in Toronto, 1972–76) has a dramatic exterior skin made of gold leaf laminated onto glass panels; this causes the colour of the towers to change throughout the day.

The **Canadian Centre for Architecture** (Montreal, 1985–89). The restoration of the Second Empire–style Shaughnessy house is in the centre and a new building surrounds it on three sides. Its limestone walls echo the walls of the Victorian row-houses in the neighbourhood.

COMING FULL CIRCLE

A postmodern period in architecture began in the mid-1970s. It was a reaction to the severity and monotony of modern architecture, rather than a specific style. Architects continued to take advantage of new materials, but they turned back once again to different periods in the past for inspiration. A new respect for the past also extends to preserving and restoring old buildings.

The **National Archives** (Gatineau, Quebec, 1994–97) houses the precious public records and historical documents of our country. Forty-eight concrete vaults containing national treasures and memories are surrounded by an outer shell of glass and steel that controls temperature and humidity. It has been built to last five hundred years. The massive columns along the front remind us of a Greek temple.

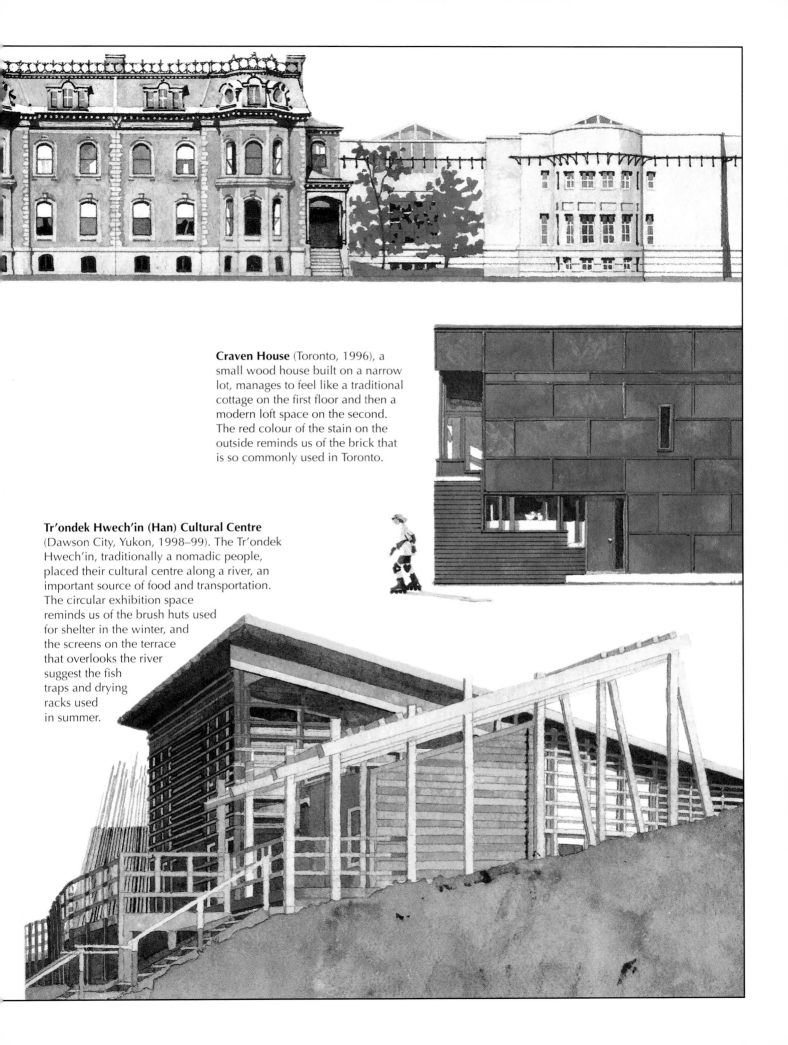

Craven House (Toronto, 1996), a small wood house built on a narrow lot, manages to feel like a traditional cottage on the first floor and then a modern loft space on the second. The red colour of the stain on the outside reminds us of the brick that is so commonly used in Toronto.

Tr'ondek Hwech'in (Han) Cultural Centre (Dawson City, Yukon, 1998–99). The Tr'ondek Hwech'in, traditionally a nomadic people, placed their cultural centre along a river, an important source of food and transportation. The circular exhibition space reminds us of the brush huts used for shelter in the winter, and the screens on the terrace that overlooks the river suggest the fish traps and drying racks used in summer.

CONCLUSION

I t is interesting that the culture of the Native peoples of Canada, who lived on this land for at least twelve thousand years before Europeans arrived, is now having influence on architectural design. Since we have the means to control nature in so many ways, we feel a new appreciation for its beauty and a closer affinity for the land. This last building is the Seabird Island School, built for the Salish band council in British Columbia. It seems to grow directly out of the ground. Its free-form roof echoes the surrounding mountains and deflects fierce winter winds. The shingled roof and walls recall the cedar houses of the coastal tribes, and the heavy struts remind us of the massive wood pillars that supported traditional houses.

If we keep looking at the architecture around us, we will learn a lot about ourselves, since the way we build is a reflection of our values.

GLOSSARY

arch

ALUMINUM:
a light, malleable, silvery white metal that doesn't tarnish

ARCH:
a curved structure that spans an opening

ASYMMETRY:
a structure that is dissimilar in size and shape on either side of a central line

ATRIUM:
an inner court open to the sky and surrounded by a roof

BALUSTRADE:
a series of short posts (balusters) that support a railing, usually around
a balcony, terrace, etc.

BATTLEMENT:
a parapet with alternating high and low portions, originally used for defence

BELVEDERE:
an open-roofed gallery designed to look out upon a pleasing scene

BRACKET:
a small supporting piece of stone or other material that carries
a projecting weight

BUTTRESS:
a mass of stonework or brickwork built against a wall to give it
additional strength

CAPITAL:
the head or crowning feature of a column or pillar

CHEVRON:
an ornamental moulding in the shape of a zigzag

COLUMN:
a rigid upright support or pillar, often designed in one of three styles –
Doric, Ionic, or Corinthian

CONCRETE:
a building material made from cement mixed with an aggregate (such as pebbles, crushed stone, or crushed brick), sand, and water, in specific proportions

CORNICE:
a horizontal decorative moulding that runs along the top of a building or wall

COURSE:
a continuous and usually horizontal row of bricks, stones, shingles, etc.,
in a wall or roof

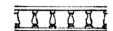

balustrade

bracket

Doric

Ionic

Corinthian

capital

chevron

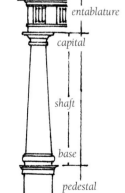

battlement

buttress

column

entablature

capital

shaft

base

pedestal

CRÉPI:
a lime plaster used on the walls of stone buildings, particularly in New France, for protection from the weather

CREST:
an ornamental finish along the top of a screen, wall, or roof

CURTAIN WALL:
an outside wall that is attached to the frame of a building but gives no support

DORMER WINDOW:
a window projecting from a sloping roof

dormer window

DUPLEX:
a two-storey house that has a complete separate apartment on each floor

EAVES:
the underside of a sloping roof, overhanging a wall

eaves

ENTABLATURE:
in classical architecture, a horizontal band that rests on top of columns

FANLIGHT:
a window, often semicircular, over a door or another window, with radiating bars that suggest a fan

FILIGREE:
delicate ornamental metalwork

FINIAL:
a small ornament at the top of a roof, gable, or other high projection

finial

FLYING BUTTRESS:
a buttress formed in an arch or half-arch (*see* buttress)

FRIEZE:
a decorated band that runs along the top of a wall, below the cornice

flying buttress

GABLE:
the triangular portion of a wall, enclosed by the sides of a pitched roof

gable

GARGOYLE:
a projection from a roof, wall, or tower that is carved into a grotesque figure, human or animal

HIPPED ROOF:
a roof that slopes on all four sides (also called hip roof)

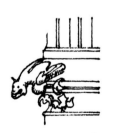

gargoyle

LOFT:
the upper floor of a warehouse

MANSARD ROOF:
a roof that has a double slope (the lower slope is very steep and the upper slope is nearly flat)

Mansard roof

pilaster

pinnacle

double sash window

shed roof

MASONRY:
stonework or brickwork

MOULDING:
the ornamentation or contouring given to cornices, etc.

PARAPET:
a low wall at the edge of a roof, balcony, bridge, or any other structure
with a sudden drop

PEDIMENT:
a triangular-shaped end of a gable, or a triangular moulding that resembles it

PILASTER:
a column projecting only slightly from a wall

PILLAR:
a free-standing upright column

PINNACLE:
the small, turret-like end of a spire, buttress, parapet, etc.

PORTICO:
a structure consisting of a roof supported by columns, usually attached
as a porch to a building

PREFABRICATE (PREFAB):
to manufacture whole buildings or their components in a factory prior
to transportation to the building site

RAFTER:
timbers or beams that support a roof

RUSTICATION:
rough-surfaced or heavily textured stonework

SASH:
in a window, the wood or metal frame that holds the glass

SEGMENTED ARCH:
an arch that has an arc smaller than a half-circle

SHED ROOF:
a roof with a single slope

SYMMETRY:
a structure that has parts of equal size and shape on either side
of a plane, line, or point

TURRET:
a small, slender tower projecting from a roof

VERANDAH:
an open gallery or porch with a roof

pointed

curved

broken   *pediments*

portico

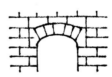
segmented arch

turret